HAUNTED CANADA

TRUE GHOST STORIES

PAT HANCOCK

SCHOLASTIC CANADA LTD.

Toronto New York London Auckland Sydney
Mexico City New Delhi Hong Kong Buenos Aires

Scholastic Canada Ltd.
175 Hillmount Road, Markham, Ontario L6C 1Z7, Canada

Scholastic Inc.
557 Broadway, New York, NY 10012, USA

Scholastic Australia Pty Limited
PO Box 579, Gosford, NSW 2250, Australia

Scholastic New Zealand Limited
Private Bag 94407, Greenmount, Auckland, New Zealand

Scholastic Ltd.
Villiers House, Clarendon Avenue, Leamington Spa,
Warwickshire CV32 5PR, UK

National Library of Canada Cataloguing in Publication
Hancock, Pat
Haunted Canada : true ghost stories / Pat Hancock.
ISBN 0-7791-1410-8
1. Ghosts—Canada. I. Title.
BF1472.C3H35 2003   133.1'0971   C2003-901064-3

Interior illustrations by Andrej Krystoforski
Illustrations copyright © 2003 by Scholastic Canada Ltd.
Cover photo © copyright Horst Klemm/Masterfile

8 7 6   Printed in Canada   05 06 07 08 09

*To my Ottawa Valley cousins and their father,
my Uncle Joe, whom I heard getting up one
morning about a month after he died.*

INTRODUCTION

Are there really ghosts? Who knows. Do I believe in them? Probably not.

But I do believe that some people — ordinary, sane, truthful people — have seen, heard, felt and even smelled some very strange things. They've seen wispy apparitions drifting past a window or hovering over a golf course. They've heard heavy footsteps or a piano playing in an empty room. They've felt the touch of an icy hand when there was no one near them, and they've smelled roses when no flowers were in bloom.

How do we refer to places where spooky things like that happen? For lack of a better explanation, we usually say they're haunted. And what causes these spooky happenings? Many people would say ghosts do.

As I said before, I don't know if there really are ghosts. But I do know that there are true stories — not the made-up kind that I also like to write — about ghosts and haunted places. They're true in the sense that the people who've told them over the years were just describing the strange, often scary things that they saw, heard, felt or smelled. Those are the kinds of stories you're about to read here.

It's good to remember, though, that you have to pay to get into some places that are reported to be haunted. Could it be that a few of the ghost stories related to them are made to sound spookier than they really are, just to attract visitors? Maybe. Maybe not. After all, rumours that a place is haunted might scare people away too.

So read on, and see for yourself just how haunted Canada is!

THE APRIL GHOST

Oak Bay, Victoria, British Columbia

The young woman startled George Drysdale. He hadn't seen her coming but, suddenly, there she was, standing just a few metres away on the golf course, with her arms reaching out to him. Drysdale was frightened. He turned to get away from her, but there she was again, standing right in front of him. Frantic, Drysdale changed direction several times, but no matter which way he turned, she was there, facing him, dressed in white and looking terribly sad. Then, as suddenly as she'd appeared, she was gone.

Taking a few deep breaths to release the terror that had been building inside him, Drysdale headed back to where his sister and her friends were standing. They had seen him trying to avoid the woman in white, and were

1

wondering what had been going on. After he told them what had happened, they agreed that no human being could move as fast as she had. So who was the woman they had all seen? They could think of only one possible explanation for the eerie event on that moonlit spring night — George Drysdale of Toronto, visiting his sister in Victoria, had just met up with the April Ghost.

The ghost got her nickname because ever since 1936 people have reported seeing her in early spring — most often in April. She's also been dubbed the Golf Course Ghost because she's usually seen walking across the Royal Victoria Golf Course, near the ocean's edge. Every now and then she has also been spotted on a nearby road that winds along the coast. The ghostly young woman usually wears a long white dress that, to some, looks like an old-fashioned wedding dress. The dress's outlines are fuzzy, giving her a spooky, rather wispy look.

The April Ghost has been seen moving about on the golf course as early as 5 p.m., but she seems to prefer visiting late in the evening — an hour or two before midnight. Her scariest appearances have her materializing suddenly, rushing up to someone as if looking for help or warning the person about some nearby danger and then melting into thin air. George Drysdale seems to have met her doing this over and over again.

But why would such a restless spirit haunt a calm, quiet place like a golf course? Perhaps the answer to that question may be found in the golf course's past, when the body of a woman was found there, buried in a sand trap. The dead woman was identified as a nurse named Doris Gravelin, and she had been brutally strangled. She had last been seen walking on the golf course with her husband, Victor, the evening before she was killed.

Doris and Victor were known to have fought a lot, and were not living together at the time of her death. Right from the start, police saw Victor as their prime suspect, but they never got to charge him with his wife's murder. While they were building a case against him, he drowned himself in the waters of Oak Bay, just along the shore by the golf course. Not long after, reports started coming in about a mysterious woman in white haunting the area.

Local believers say Doris must be the April Ghost. But is she running to people for help or warning them to stay away from a place where such terrible things happened? Both theories are popular, and there is even a third idea about what she's up to. According to some, it's usually couples who aren't married that report seeing her as George Drysdale did: rushing forward with outstretched arms and then disappearing. Perhaps she is trying to warn couples about the dangers of a bad marriage, like her own.

THE NIGHTMARE KNOTS

Montreal, Quebec

The year was 1929. The place was a house in Montreal on Rue Ste. Famille, just west of Boulevard St. Laurent and north of de Maisonneuve. To passersby, the house looked perfectly normal. There was no outward sign of the bizarre things going on inside, and the people that lived there were too afraid to tell anyone about their troubles.

Eventually a reporter learned what was happening on Rue Ste. Famille, but even then the adults in the house insisted he not include their names when his story was published. After all, they were being troubled by knots. Who would believe that knots could be scary?

The knots started to appear without any warning that there was a troubling presence in the house. Knotted sleeves in sweaters were a nuisance, but could have been a practical joke — even if the prankster refused to own up to his or her handiwork. The knots in the towels were annoying; the ones in the curtains even more so, because they left behind unattractive wrinkles that had to be ironed out. Soon small, tightly twisted knots were appearing everywhere in the house — in sheets, pillowcases, tablecloths and dishtowels, in socks, shirts, dresses and trousers.

The parents were frantic. They spied on their children, hoping to catch a young culprit in the act. They even found themselves spying on each other. When they were absolutely certain that no family member was tying the knots, they did the only thing they could think of to bring them peace. They asked two priests to come and bless the house. But despite the priests' efforts, the knots continued to appear. Finally, feeling desperate, the family called in the police.

The police were intrigued with the mystery. They carefully examined the many knotted items, questioned everyone in turn and searched the house thoroughly from top to bottom. While searching the basement, one officer detected an unpleasant odour of decay. Could it be, he wondered, that a body had been buried there, and the dead person's ghost was tying the knots so that someone would look for the body? Armed with shovels and pick-axes, the police poked about and dug up much of the basement, but found no evidence of a crime or a corpse.

Another police officer came up with an experiment to make sure no human was tying the knots. Officers left several handkerchiefs in one of the rooms, and locked and sealed the door behind them. When they broke the seal and unlocked the door the next morning, they were amazed to find the cloth squares twisted into tiny knots.

Next they decided to have every member of the family tie knots in several different items. Then they studied all the knots carefully. What they learned surprised them. The knots appearing throughout the house looked just like those tied by the youngest child. The police figured she must have been tying the knots in some sort of trance-like state, with no memory in her conscious mind of what she was doing. From their point of view, the case was finally closed. Curiously enough, the knots stopped appearing not long after their investigation ended.

But the parents were never convinced that the police had truly solved the mystery. From their point of view, their young daughter couldn't possibly have been the phantom knotter without their knowing it, and the police should have felt the same way. They were the ones who had sealed the room with the handkerchiefs in it. And they were the ones who had found the seal still intact the next morning, with the handkerchiefs all tied up inside.

Did a ghostly double of the young girl haunt the house for those few months in 1929? It seems a little hard to believe. But that explanation makes at least as much sense as the one put forward by the police, especially in light of the results of their own experiment. According to them, no human, not even a child, could have entered that sealed room.

OTHERWORLDLY ENCORE

Winnipeg, Manitoba

Laurence Irving was the son of Sir Henry Irving, a famous Victorian actor. Sir Henry was the first actor ever to be honoured with a knighthood. Like his father, Laurence was also a talented stage performer. So was Laurence's wife, Mabel Hackney. After starring in a play in Winnipeg in May 1914, the popular British couple took the train east to Quebec. There they boarded the ocean liner *Empress of Ireland* to return home to England.

On the evening of May 29, while the *Empress of Ireland* was still in the St. Lawrence River, it was rammed by a Norwegian ship. In just 14 minutes the *Empress* sank, claiming the lives of 1014 passengers and crew. Laurence Irving and Mabel Hackney were the two most famous passengers to die so tragically that night.

Actors Mabel Hackney and Laurence Irving

There are those who say the ghosts of Irving and Hackney never left Canada, but stayed on where the actors had given their last performances — at the Walker Theatre in Winnipeg. Built in 1906, the theatre was recently renamed after singer Burton Cummings. It has more than 1600 seats and is home to many performing arts events. It is also a place where creepy things happen; things that some people blame on the spirits of the two famous actors.

Hearing applause in a theatre isn't scary; it's expected. But what if it's coming from rows of empty seats? That's been reported at the theatre. So has the opening and closing of heavy steel doors. Who was clapping? Who was pushing and pulling on the doors? Who kept shutting dressing room doors after the night watchman made sure they were open? Are Irving and Hackney moving around the theatre, still giving encores so many years after their final bows?

One security guard wouldn't find the idea of ghostly actors at the Burton Cummings Theatre such a far-fetched idea. After all, it was he who finally wedged the dressing room doors open, only to find the wedges kicked out and the doors closed the next time he checked the halls. He's also the one who reported that his normally friendly, lively dogs would behave quite strangely when making nightly rounds with him. Instead of straining to get ahead of him, they would often press up against his legs as if frightened by something. They would also suddenly start barking for no obvious reason.

Maybe the dogs could hear or sense what an investigative reporter's tape recorder picked up one night, when human ears detected nothing. Although the theatre was empty, a recorder left running for a couple of hours captured sounds of footsteps, hammering and even a few whispers. One of the whispers sounded very much like someone saying, "Please . . ."

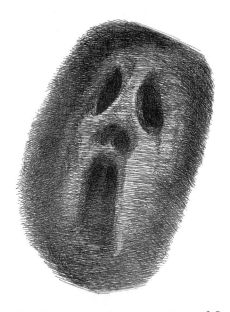

THE MOTORCYCLE GHOST

Lake Scugog, Ontario

Scugog Island is a big island in Lake Scugog about 65 kilometres northeast of Toronto. On the island is a road that ends at a farmer's field. It's been officially named Ghost Road. A romantic spot, especially on a moonlit night, it has quite a reputation as a lovers' lane. But many young people who find their way there aren't really looking for privacy. They know they're likely to find quite a few cars at the end of Ghost Road, all with their lights off and all parked facing south. It's a strange scene, and between 11 p.m. and 2 a.m. it often gets stranger. That's when the ghostly white light usually appears.

More often than not, those waiting to see the light aren't disappointed. It has been appearing for over four decades, on at least 200 nights of the year. It's more likely to materialize in October and November, the months on either side of Halloween. At first the light appears off in the distance, towards the south end of the field. Over the next minute or so it bounces along just above the ground, moving in a northeast direction, coming closer and closer to anyone waiting to see it. Then, just before the light disappears, there's a brief flash of a small red light trailing behind it. Not everyone sees the red light, but some people have seen the white light as many as ten times in one night. It's not unusual for it to appear at least twice in the same evening.

For years now people have tried to find the source of the light. Police have investigated it; traffic inspectors have checked it out. Even airport officials have looked into a possible cause. Some daring young men have run after it on foot; others have foolishly tried chasing it down in their cars. Officially, the cause of the light remains a mystery.

But according to local lore, the unofficial explanation is to be found in a tragic tale of death. One version of the story has the accident happening back in the 1950s to a teenager named Sweeney. A more specific account says it happened in 1963 to an unnamed youth. Both stories tell of a carefree young man riding his motorcycle across the fields late at night. In the darkness he didn't see the fence wire, and so, when he hit it at top speed, he was decapitated.

Ever since then people have seen the light. And ever since then, night after night, young people gather to wait for the appearance of Sweeney, headless, forever racing his motorcycle across the field at the end of Ghost Road.

THE BLOODSTAIN IN THE ATTIC

Calgary, Alberta

Deane House was built in 1906 for Richard Burton Deane, Fort Calgary's North West Mounted Police Superintendent. Over the years the stately house has also served as a railway agent's home, a boarding house, and a gallery and studio space for local artists. But during the late 1980s and early 1990s, many people weren't too comfortable staying at Deane House. And who could blame them? Most of us wouldn't want to stick around a place full of mysterious noises, where chairs and dishes might suddenly start flying around and smashing to the ground.

But why were such spooky things happening at Deane House? During the time that the building was a rundown, neglected rooming house, several of its tenants were brutally murdered, and others committed suicide. Could it be that the ghosts of these unfortunate souls were haunting the place? Some people thought so.

A religious ceremony performed at the house in the mid-1990s seemed to have a calming effect. Deane House was renovated again and over the years has been transformed into a cozy restaurant with a great view of the Elbow River. But it looks as if hungry diners aren't the only ones who find the atmosphere there welcoming. According to several eyewitnesses, some very strange things still happen at Deane House; things that suggest otherworldly spirits may still be hanging around.

First there's the matter of the mysterious woman in white. She appears in the attic every now and then. Is she the ghost of a former boarder whose husband stabbed her and then killed himself? Robert Jensen, a Deane House supervisor, thinks she could be. That might also explain the red patch in the attic. Jensen says it looks very much like a bloodstain, adding that it changes colour — from fresh-blood red to dried-blood brown — depending on what time of the year it is.

Then there are the phantoms that open and close doors and windows, toss small items into the air and grab and hide things when you turn away for a second. Jensen thinks the ghosts of Deane House do stuff like this when they're bored. Apparently boredom has also driven them to make an antique phone that no longer works start ringing as if it were new. And invisible hands have been known to poke at the keys on an old typewriter on display in a small den.

Some people think tales of ghosts at Deane House are simply that — tall tales intended to attract more customers to the restaurant. But when one lunch guest made that point to a staff member, her teacup started drifting up above the table. The woman accused staff of playing a trick on her, but, try as she might, she couldn't figure out how they could have pulled it off.

One waitress felt so uncomfortable working there that she quit after just a few months. Smelling pipe tobacco and hearing laughter in empty rooms made her nervous, but staying around to lock up at the end of the day was even spookier. When she had to turn off the lights on the upper floor and walk downstairs, she felt as if she were being followed so closely that she could feel someone's breath on her neck. After being left to lock up a few times, she decided it was time to start job-hunting again.

Robert Jensen admits that the ghostly goings-on gave him the jitters at first too. But rather than being scared off, he says "Good morning, ghosties" when he comes to work, and he ends each day with an equally friendly goodnight to the phantoms of Deane House.

Deane House

GHOSTS IN THE RIGGING

Mahone Bay, Nova Scotia

Privateering was a dangerous way to make a living, but it could also be a quick way to make a fortune. When countries were at war, their governments would give permission to some private ship owners to attack enemy merchant ships and claim any loot they found for themselves. Doing this allowed the navy to spend more time fighting sea battles, and it robbed the enemy of needed supplies carried by the merchant ships.

During the War of 1812 several American privateers chased down British ships sailing along the southeastern coast of Nova Scotia. But on June 27, 1813, one of those American ships, the *Young Teazer*, became the hunted instead of the hunter.

A British navy warship chased the *Young Teazer* into

Mahone Bay west of Halifax. A British deserter aboard the *Young Teazer*, realizing that his ship was trapped and about to be boarded by British officers, made a desperate move. Knowing that if they found him he'd be hanged, he threw a lit torch into the ship's supply of gunpowder.

The fiery explosion that followed blew apart the *Young Teazer* and killed many of the crew. Some of the sailors were buried in the nearby town of Chester, and parts of the ship not destroyed by fire were hauled ashore to be used as building materials.

About a year later, a ghost ship made its first of many appearances near Chester in Mahone Bay.

Ever since then, hundreds of people have seen a burning ship out on the bay. Some of them were in their own boats when the ship appeared out of nowhere. At times it seemed to be heading right for them, and they were terrified that it was going to run them down. At the last second, it vanished into thin air. Sometimes it passes so close to the shore that people on the beach can see the sailors up in the rigging. In most cases the ship appears to be on fire, which is why so many people believe it is the ghost of the *Young Teazer*. Over the years, some people have even reported hearing the tortured cries of the men who have been trying to escape the burning ship for more than a century.

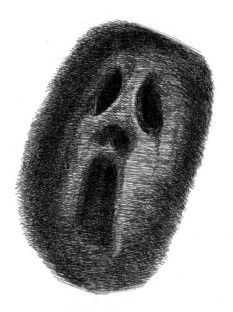

LAKESIDE HORROR

Red Deer Point, Manitoba

It was the second week of March 1898. Five men — three Canadians and two Norwegians — had taken the train from Winnipeg to Winnipegosis Station. From there they had travelled by wagon to an isolated fishing camp on Lake Winnipegosis, near Red Deer Point. The camp's buildings were sturdily built and well-stocked with everything needed to make the men's stay a pleasant one. When they arrived, they were looking forward to a week or two of good company and great fishing. By Wednesday, March 9, they were beginning to think they should never have left Winnipeg.

Details of what happened became public when one of the men — a Mr. A.C. O'Beirne — sent a letter from the camp to the *Winnipeg Free Press*. Strange as the story seemed, the newspaper's editor decided to print it on March 17. After all, Mr. O'Beirne was well known in the community. He wasn't the kind of person to make up such a terrifying tale and claim it to be true.

According to O'Beirne, a loud scratching sound at a window on Wednesday evening was the first sign of some otherworldly force at work. That noise, together with pipes banging and the sound of something being dragged across the roof, started around 9 p.m. and kept the men awake until about midnight. And, as O'Beirne pointed out in his letter, "We could find nothing to account for these noises, though we did our best to do so."

On Thursday evening, a small bell started ringing. At first its tinkling seemed to be coming from the stable. After a while it seemed to move closer to the main building and then, right inside. Again, the men couldn't find the source of the ringing. Worse still, the scratching, banging and dragging started up too.

Those spooky noises weren't all that invaded the men's peace and quiet Friday night. That evening, tin dishes were flung off the shelves onto the floor, and boots and overshoes were whipped across the room. A few men from a nearby lumber camp were on hand that night, and they too witnessed the nightmarish sights and sounds.

O'Beirne's description of what happened Saturday is chilling. As well as the scratching, banging, dragging and ringing, O'Beirne told of a heavy iron stove lid being lifted and thrown on the floor, a ladle being tossed out of a pot and then put back in it, and one man's hat flying off a nail onto his head. The paper O'Beirne was writing on was snatched out from under his hand, and the table he was working at began to shake.

Around 10:30 p.m., the lamp blew out and, as

O'Beirne put it, "Pandemonium let loose. Everything in the camp seemed to be on the move. The blows on the window were delivered with apparently sledgehammer force, the stoves rattled and shook . . . and there was also a loud knocking at the door. This happened three times, and then gradually the disturbances became less and ceased as usual shortly before midnight."

O'Beirne ended his letter with a plea to readers to come up with some sort of reasonable explanation for what happened at the fishing camp. But the best explanation anyone could offer was that the camp had been haunted by a poltergeist.

Poltergeist comes from two German words — *poltern*, meaning "to knock," and *Geist*, which means "spirit." The term poltergeist refers to mischievous, sometimes mean, spirits that do things like make strange noises, shake and rattle furniture and windows, snatch and grab small items and send objects flying around a room. Poltergeists are usually active at night, and after a few days or weeks, they seem to stop what they're doing as suddenly as they started.

That certainly sounds like what happened on Lake Winnipegosis back in March of 1898. Still, would O'Beirne have thought poltergeist haunting was a reasonable explanation for what he and his fishing companions saw and heard? Who knows. But simply naming the type of spirit that may have haunted the camp wouldn't have made the experience any less terrifying for the men who suffered through it. Poltergeist or not — it had scared the wits out of them.

THE HAUNTED HOTEL

Banff, Alberta

Each year thousands of tourists from around the world travel to Banff, Alberta, attracted by its incredible natural beauty. And those who can afford to often stay at the luxurious Banff Springs Hotel. Built high in the Rockies in the 1880s, the hotel offers spectacular views of the snow-capped mountains and the Bow River valley. Outside it looks like an old Scottish castle. Inside it provides guests with every possible comfort. Many people like the hotel so much they say they wish they didn't have to leave. Some people believe that a few individuals have decided to stay on forever, even in death.

Over the years there have been several reports of ghostly sightings at the "castle in the Rockies." A mysterious bartender is said to occasionally appear in the bar to tell patrons who've had too much to drink they should call it a night and go to bed. There have also been tales of a wandering bagpiper who might be looking for what he's lost — namely his head. But most reports about seeing phantoms involve two ghosts in particular.

The first is said to be a regular at the hotel. He's even been given a name — Sam. While Sam seems to prefer hanging around on the hotel's ninth floor, he's been spotted in many different areas of the building. Guests who claim to have met up with Sam report seeing a man wearing an old-fashioned bellhop's uniform. But Sam doesn't just look like a bellhop; he acts like one too. Always polite and helpful, he's carried bags for guests and opened doors for a few who have locked themselves out of their rooms. But as soon as someone tries to chat with him or offer him a tip for his services, he leaves so quickly it's as if he disappeared.

Guests' descriptions of Sam and his uniform suggest he might be a bellhop who worked at the hotel more than 70 years ago, but no one knows for sure. One thing is certain, though — there's no real person who looks like Sam working at the hotel.

The second phantom that several people have seen drifting around the hotel is an unnamed woman wearing a flowing white gown. Hers is a tragic story. It's said that she is the ghost of a beautiful young bride whose family had booked the grand ballroom for a magnificent wedding party. As she started walking down the marble staircase with her new husband to join their guests, she tripped on the long train of her dress. Another version of the story says her gown brushed against candles on the stairs and caught fire, and she stumbled as she whirled around to stamp out the flames. Either way, her husband tried desperately to

Banff Springs Hotel

stop her from falling, but she broke her neck as she tumbled down the stairs and fell dead on the floor below.

Does the spirit of that young bride really haunt the hotel where she died? Banff Springs representatives say no, adding that the sad tale was started as a public relations prank decades ago. But over the years a few people have mentioned feeling an icy breeze slip past them as they walked down the marble staircase. Others claim to have caught a passing glimpse of a young woman in white coming down the stairs. And still others say that they've seen, just for an instant, a vision of a beautiful girl in a flowing white dress, waltzing alone across the grand ballroom floor.

THE GHOST TRAPPER

Eastern Labrador,
Newfoundland and Labrador

It's said that some ghostly spirits are doomed to wander the earth forever, unable to find peace after death because of the terrible things they did while they were alive. That notion is often put forward to explain the haunting appearances of the Ghost Trapper of Labrador. Also known as Smoker, the mysterious trapper is usually identified as Esau Dillingham, a Newfoundlander who moved to mainland Labrador in the early 1900s.

He'd come in search of better hunting grounds, but after running his new trap lines for a year or so, Dillingham decided there had to be an easier way to make a living. He became a bootlegger and cooked up his illegal alcohol in a backwoods still. Then he peddled it around to willing and eager buyers. It was disgusting tasting stuff, nicknamed smoke by the locals, who started calling its maker Smoker. It was also a potent brew; so much so that it was often poisonous. More than a few men went crazy drinking the stuff. For some, it was lethal.

Eventually the RCMP caught up with Smoker, but he didn't change his ways. After spending a year in jail in St. John's, he went right back to running a still and selling his illegal booze. But he was better at it this time. He rounded up a team of snow-white dogs, painted his wooden sled white and made himself a parka and pants from white furs and skins.

The camouflage worked. As Dillingham roamed the coast of Labrador selling his deadly drink, he blended in perfectly with the snowy drifts and blizzard-driven whiteouts. The police couldn't catch him and the money rolled in. But a lot of good it did him. Smoker had taken to drinking his own smoke.

As the madness crept in, Smoker lost control. One version of the story has him arrested in 1920 for murdering a customer, and then falling in his jail cell and breaking his back. Another version has him staggering around on a fish-drying rack, or flake, and breaking his back in a fall from the flake. Either way, a fall killed him. But just before he died, his head filling with searing visions of hellish torment, he prayed to be spared eternal punishment. He prayed for the chance to keep driving his dog team after death so he could make up for all the bad things he had done.

After Smoker's death, a few people reported hearing the sounds of a dog team being urged on by its driver. When they looked outside, they saw nothing and there were no sled or dog tracks in the snow. Others reported seeing a mysterious sledder dressed in white racing across the snow-covered landscape. Both types of appearances seemed to occur just before a severe storm blew in. Was it Smoker's ghost, trying to warn people to take shelter from an approaching blizzard? Some people thought so.

There are other stories of the ghostly trapper doing good deeds. One involves a lost hunter who was guided to safety during a blustery storm by a large man dressed all in white. Another involves two RCMP officers on patrol in Labrador in 1949. Supposedly the Mounties, lost in a blizzard, were dangerously close to freezing to death. With barely enough strength left to urge on their husky dogs, the men despaired of ever making it back to headquarters. Suddenly, another man appeared in the distance. He was dressed all in white and he was driving a team of 14 white dogs pulling a white sled. The Mounties decided to follow him.

Two agonizing hours later, almost blinded by snow and ready to drop with exhaustion, the Mounties came upon a cabin where some trappers had taken shelter from the storm. They staggered inside, assuming their rescuer had done the same because they had lost sight of him outdoors. But he wasn't there, and the trappers told them he never would be. They told the Mounties they had been saved by Smoker, a murderer whom other lawmen had brought to justice nearly 30 years earlier.

Was that dramatic rescue one more example of the Ghost Trapper of Labrador keeping his deathbed promise to do good in the afterlife? Maybe, but there are problems with the Ghost Trapper story. For one thing, the Newfoundland Rangers patrolled Labrador from 1935 to 1950. The Royal Canadian Mounted Police didn't assume law enforcement duties in Newfoundland and Labrador until 1950, a year after Newfoundland joined Confederation.

Moreover, before 1935 no one force was responsible for policing most of Labrador. It seems highly unlikely that members of the Newfoundland Constabulary would have crossed the Strait of Belle Isle to chase a bootlegger all over the mainland during winter storms and drag him back to a St. John's jail. And if Smoker had murdered someone, wouldn't there be an official record of that crime? You would think so.

So what part, if any, of the Ghost Trapper story is fact? It's hard to say. What does seem to be true is that every now and then, someone caught a glimpse of a mysterious figure dressed in white, driving a team of white dogs that pulled a white wooden sled. And any unexplained events that happened next have only fed the legend of the ghostly bootlegger who seeks redemption.

THAT REBEL SPIRIT

Toronto, Ontario

William Lyon Mackenzie was a crusading newspaper editor and publisher, a fiery provincial politician, Toronto's
first mayor and leader of the Rebellion of 1837 in Upper
Canada (now Ontario). That's an impressive list of accom-
plishments, and one that would probably have brought
most people not only fame, but fortune too. But
Mackenzie was an honest man. He never took bribes and
he never accepted government money for jobs he didn't
do. All his life he fought that sort of corruption, and all his
life he struggled to make ends meet.

After the government crushed the rebellion, Mackenzie
had to escape to the United States to avoid imprisonment
or, worse still, a date with the gallows. During the next 12
years in exile, he tried to make enough money to care for

his family by writing, taking odd jobs and publishing a few small newspapers. In 1849, when he was pardoned and allowed to return to Canada, he came back to Toronto.

Mackenzie went right back to attacking government corruption as both a newspaper publisher and an elected politician. However, he wasn't nearly as popular as he had been in the 1830s and, over the years, he found it harder and harder to survive, both politically and financially. In 1858, tired, in poor health and in debt, he resigned from the legislative assembly of Upper Canada. Faithful friends, who hadn't forgotten how hard he had fought for just causes, raised enough money to provide him and his family with a furnished house. Mackenzie died there three years later, in 1861.

The house, at 82 Bond Street, was rescued from the wrecker's ball in 1936 and was gradually restored to look as it did when Mackenzie lived in it. It's now a museum with many of his belongings on display. There's even a printing press like the one he used set up in the basement. It's still in working condition, but back in 1960, Mr. and Mrs. Alex Dobban, live-in caretakers at the house, had every reason to wish it weren't. Every now and then, when they were alone in the place, they would hear the press rumbling away in the basement. They also heard footsteps pacing around the house and the piano playing all on its own. The Dobbans moved out after only a few months of this, and from then on the building's caretakers lived outside of the house.

But the incidents that made the Dobbans nervous were minor compared to what had happened to the caretaking couple that came before them. Mr. and Mrs. Charles Edmunds lived in a third-floor apartment of Mackenzie House from 1956 to 1960. It was only four years, but for

Mackenzie House

Mrs. Edmunds, her time there was almost more than she could bear. She learned to put up with the mysterious footsteps, and wasn't too frightened by the rumbling noises in the basement and the rocking chair that moved back and forth as if there were someone in it. But she found the apparitions to be very disturbing.

Several times she caught sight of a long-haired woman in an old-fashioned dress wandering the halls. Occasionally she encountered a short, bald man wearing a nineteenth-century style jacket. Her description of the man was eerily similar to Mackenzie's appearance, except for his baldness. But the rebel leader's famed red hair was actually the product of a skilled wigmaker. Mackenzie had turned to wigs when he lost most of his hair, but maybe he felt comfortable enough at home to leave his wig on the dressing table, and his spirit felt the same way.

But it was a second long-haired woman who truly terrified Mrs. Edmunds. The first time she appeared, Mrs. Edmunds was in bed. She'd been asleep for a couple of hours when a touch on her shoulder woke her up. She looked up to find a woman looming above her. The woman appeared to be standing between the wall and the head-board — a space too narrow for any human being to fit. Her long brown hair dangled down near Mrs. Edmunds' pillow. Then suddenly, the woman disappeared.

The ghostly apparition stayed away for a year, but when she reappeared, she did so in a most dramatic fashion. Once again she woke up Mrs. Edmunds, hovering over her from above the headboard. But this time, before she faded away, she reached down and hit Mrs. Edmunds in the face. Mr. Edmunds comforted his hysterical wife and coaxed her back to sleep by saying she'd just had a bad dream. But Mrs. Edmunds knew better. When she woke up the next morning, one side of her face was sore, and when she looked in the mirror she saw why. Her eye was red with broken blood vessels, and a dark bruise was forming around it.

After the Dobbans moved out in 1960, a minister performed a religious service to drive the otherworldly spirits from the house. After that the haunting incidents seemed to stop. Some people said reports of ghostly visitations had been invented to attract visitors to the historical museum. But no one could convince Mrs. Edmunds that what had happened to her had just been a publicity stunt. Her black eye was all the proof she needed that something spooky and strange had been going on at Mackenzie House, something she was very relieved to be done with when she and her husband moved out.

THiNGS THAT GO BUMP iN THE NiGHT

Kenosee Lake, Saskatchewan

Nestled on the southeastern edge of Moose Mountain Provincial Park, Kenosee Lake is a popular summer resort with impressive scenery, good fishing and great campsites. And for those who are looking for some other-worldly entertainment, it's also said to have a haunted nightclub.

For more than ten years now, folks have been talking about the spooky things that happened at the Moosehead Inn, a former dance hall that was once a favourite hang-out for teenagers.

In 1990, Estevan resident Dale Orsted bought the inn and decided to fix it up a little. But he'd only had the place a few months when he started noticing that things like ashtrays, cutlery, glasses and figurines were disappearing at an unusual rate.

At first Orsted thought a few customers or staff members might be suffering from a bad case of sticky fingers. But the missing items started showing up again, often in the weirdest places. Then the loud noises started. Banging on the locked front door, thumping on the floors overhead — the racket could last for hours. Frustrated and frightened, Orsted called the police, but they couldn't figure out who or what was causing it.

In 1992, things went from bad to worse. One night, after the last customers had left, Orsted and a friend began ripping up some smelly old carpeting. Almost immediately the noises started up again, this time louder than ever. Sounds of large metal objects crashing into each other were so loud they nearly shattered the windowpanes.

The ear-splitting, nerve-jarring clanging and banging went on all week, night after night, until all the new carpeting was installed. Until then, Orsted had laughed whenever anyone suggested his place might be haunted. After that harrowing week, he found himself — against his better judgment — agreeing with them.

The presence of a ghost could also explain other things that started happening at the Moosehead. The lights flickered several times a night, the dishwasher turned itself on and off, a pail flew across the dance floor, and locked security doors suddenly crashed open and slammed shut. Patrons were excited to be around when some of these things happened, but they were a little nervous too. So was Orsted. He'd been living at the inn since he bought it, but for two years in the mid-1990s he moved back to Estevan, commuting to work each day just so he could get a break from all the stress he felt at Kenosee Lake.

As word about the Moosehead's troubles spread, Canadian and American TV crews showed up to film the story of the haunted inn, and investigative reporters wrote about the creepy incidents experienced by Orsted, his girl-friend, his buddies and the servers working there. A psychic who read about the haunting phoned Orsted and told him his renovations to the place had probably upset the original owner, Archibald Grandison. She said that the old gentleman's spirit was most likely the source of the mournful moaning sound Orsted had started hearing outside his bedroom door.

Finally Orsted decided to take an "if you can't beat 'em, join 'em" approach to his weird predicament. He came up with the idea of hosting a psychic fair at the inn. Several people interested in ghosts and the paranormal showed up for the fair, which turned out to be quite an entertaining event for the whole town.

During the fair, Orsted took part in a special gathering, or seance, organized by a psychic who said she detected three separate ghosts at the inn. She claimed she was able to convince two of them — a cleaning woman and a teenaged boy who had drowned — to leave. But a third — an older man who may have been Archibald Grandison — seemed determined to stay around until he was certain his widow was being well cared for.

Mrs. Grandison was Orsted's next-door neighbour. He liked the elderly lady, and was already keeping a friendly eye her, so he didn't mind at all making more of an effort to look after her. As soon as he started doing that, the number of spooky incidents decreased dramatically. In 1999, when Mrs. Grandison died, the ghost — and Orsted — finally found peace.

THE FIERY PHANTOM SHIP

Northumberland Strait, Prince Edward Island

You've just spent a perfectly wonderful day on one of Prince Edward Island's sun-drenched beaches, just along the Northumberland Strait. You're packing up the picnic basket when you see it — a large ship, sails billowing. It appears out of nowhere and seems to be sailing dangerously close to shore. You stare in amazement as you realize it's on fire. Then, as quickly as it appeared, it's gone.

If this happened to you, you would join the ranks of hundreds, maybe even thousands of others who have spotted a mysterious three-masted schooner sailing the waters off the southern shores of PEI. Your sighting would be a bit unusual because most appearances occur in the autumn, not in the summer, and often just before a stormy northeast wind blows in, not at the end of a warm, sunny day. But ever since the 1780s, the phantom ship has sailed into view in the spring, summer, winter and fall, in good and bad weather alike.

At times the schooner has even sailed right into Charlottetown Harbour, in clear view of scores of people working on the docks. Once, about a hundred years ago, several dockhands jumped into a dinghy and furiously rowed out to rescue the sailors they could see fighting the fires on deck. But just as they were about to reach the burning schooner, it was swallowed up in a murky mist. When the mist cleared just minutes later, no trace of the ship or its crew could be found.

It's easy enough to write off one person's story of the ship as the work of an overactive imagination, but reports from groups of witnesses such as those would-be rescuers in the harbour are much harder to ignore. Fifty years later a carload of teenagers spotted the ship in Victoria Harbour. They saw the crew moving around on deck and climbing up and down the rigging. They also saw the fires burning, but they watched long enough to note that the flames never consumed the ship. And in the early 1960s, people on a crowded beach were amazed when the burning schooner appeared late one afternoon.

No one story — a pirate's ship sunk off the coast, a vessel loaded with immigrants lost in a storm, a ship weighted down with lumber that disappeared without a trace — satisfies people's efforts to explain the presence of the ship in the area. But, together with the eerie sounds of cannon fire or "sea guns" that are often heard in the distance, the appearance of the phantom ship in the Northumberland Strait can still send shivers up the spines of many Islanders.

MURDERED FOR SILENCE

Hudson, Quebec

The Willow Place Inn can be found in Hudson, Quebec, a village 40 kilometres west of Montreal on picturesque Lac des Deux Montagnes. After a fire destroyed it in 1989, the inn was completely rebuilt and furnished in the style of the eighteenth-century building that had burned down.

The original structure was built in 1820 as a family home. In 1824, François Desjardins bought it and turned the main floor into a general store. But Desjardins was more than simple shopkeeper. He was also a member of the Patriotes, and, like the others in his group, he wanted to get rid of the appointed governing council that ignored the wishes of the elected assembly in favour of the rich and powerful. By the early 1830s, talk of rebellion was in the air. By 1837, Desjardins had started stockpiling guns and

ammunition in his basement and was making his store available for secret meetings of the Patriotes who were fed up with government scandals and corruption.

At the time a young woman, Mary Kirkbride, was working as a maid in the Desjardins' home. When she overheard some of the plans the Patriotes were making to organize an armed revolt, she felt she had to warn the authorities. Some say she ran away and reported what she'd heard. But others tell a more sinister story. They believe she was killed to keep her quiet, and her body was buried in the basement.

Over the years, the second version of events seemed to provide the best explanation for the spooky goings-on in the house. After Desjardins was sent to jail for taking part in the 1837 Rebellion of Lower Canada (Quebec), the Brasseur family bought his home and turned it into a boarding house. When they sold it, it became an inn, or *auberge*. In the 1970s people in Hudson started talking publicly about the ghostly activities that had been observed at the inn for some time.

Were the Willow's owners just spreading rumours to boost business? Not according to some of the staff. They, as well as the owners, saw furniture being pushed around by an invisible force. Often they were startled and nearly tripped when the basement door slammed shut behind them. Stones were heaped in front of a door to one of the guestrooms. And, from empty rooms and deserted hallways, they smelled perfume and heard the haunting sound of a woman singing.

Incidents like these don't seem to occur as often since the inn was rebuilt. But, as in the past, disturbing events usually happen between October 31 and the end of November. Skeptics aren't surprised that the apparent haunting begins on Halloween. What better night, they ask, for someone to claim to have seen, heard or even smelled a ghost? But the phantom is restless until the end of November. Fighting between Patriotes and government forces first broke out in the area in November 1837. Were plans for those skirmishes what Mary Kirkbride overheard and tried to report? If so, she would most likely have met her fate around the same time as many Patriotes met theirs — in the month of November.

Willow Place Inn

THE RESTLESS SPIRIT

Taloyoak, Nunavut

For many centuries the Netsilik Inuit, or "people of the seal," lived in the area around the Boothia Peninsula, about 200 kilometres above the Arctic Circle. Their main source of food and clothing was seals. They also hunted caribou and polar bears.

Like other Inuit in the Arctic, the Netsilik Inuit lived a nomadic life, staying in igluvigaqs (snow dwellings) in the winter and in tents in the summer. When someone died, the body was wrapped in caribou skins. If the community was camped near the sea, the remains were slipped respectfully into the water. If the group was further inland, the body was placed under a mound of rocks, but, if there weren't enough rocks in the area, it was simply left on the land.

In 1948 the Hudson's Bay Company set up a post at the base of the Boothia Peninsula, and a new community known as Spence Bay (now Taloyoak) grew up around it. By the 1960s the government had encouraged most of the Inuit living in the area to abandon their nomadic lifestyle and move into houses in the settlement.

It's said that in the early 1950s an Inuit woman was murdered out on the land, several kilometres from Spence Bay. Instead of being buried where she had been killed, her body was brought to the Hudson's Bay Company post and kept in an unheated room there until it could be buried at the settlement in the spring. Apparently the haunting noises started soon afterwards.

Night after night, people staying at the post reported hearing a door opening and footsteps crossing the outer room toward the main living quarters. They also heard what sounded like a woman's voice, coughing and making other sounds. The first few times this happened, whoever was inside got up to see who had arrived, only to find no one was there. Eventually it became obvious that no human being was making those mysterious noises, and it seemed clear to most local residents who heard them that the ghost of the murdered woman was making her presence known.

The strange, unexplained noises stopped when the woman's remains were buried in the spring. But for years afterwards, many people continued to believe that the Hudson's Bay Company building was really and truly haunted.

POSSESSION

Amherst, Nova Scotia

Sometimes a ghost haunts a person, not a place. Wherever that person goes, spooky things happen. Ghost experts usually blame this type of haunting on a particular kind of ghost — a poltergeist. Poltergeists are mischief-makers. They hide things, make scary noises and send stuff flying around a room. They don't hang around forever and they often pester a younger person. That description matches what happened to Esther Cox, but only up to a point. The poltergeist that targeted her didn't just pester her. For nearly a year, starting in September 1878, it made her life a living hell.

Cox was 18 when the nightmare began. At the time she was living in the home of her married sister, Olive, and Olive's husband, Daniel Teed. Her brother, William, and another sister, Jane, were also staying in the two-storey wooden house in Amherst. So were Daniel and Olive's young children and Daniel's brother, John. Esther and Jane shared a bedroom in the cozy, but crowded house.

One night in early September, Jane awakened to hear Esther whispering that there were mice in their bed. At first Jane thought her sister was just imagining things. Then she heard the scratching too. When both sisters jumped out of bed, they realized the sounds were coming from under the bed, not in it. They pulled out a low cardboard box of quilt patches, figuring the little rodents were building a nest in it. But as soon as they dragged the box into the middle of the room, it seemed to take on a life of its own. It shot up in the air, then tipped over on its side. A few seconds later, it took off and fell down again.

The sisters screamed for help. Their brother-in-law, Daniel, rushed in to see what was wrong. But when he heard what had happened, he said they must have been dreaming, and told them to go back to bed. The next night, though, all of the adults in the house came running into the bedroom when Jane screamed for help. What they found nearly turned their stomachs. As Esther screamed and writhed in pain on the bed, she began to swell up like a bloated corpse. Loud raps and snapping sounds filled the air, many of them coming from under the bed. Suddenly, after one ear-splitting bang, Esther's body deflated, and the wretched young woman fell into a deep sleep.

When a similar scene played out again four nights later, Esther's family asked the doctor to pay a visit. After listening to what he thought was a lot of nonsense, he told them that Esther was just suffering from a bad case of nerves. But right after he stated his diagnosis, Esther's pillow started moving back and forth and her blankets flew off the bed and across the room. The loud noises started again, but they weren't nearly as frightening as a new, softer, scratching sound that made everyone look above the bed. There, over the headboard, words began to emerge. The message, written by the unseen force, was chilling. "Esther Cox," it read, "you are mine to kill."

Fear filled the house from then on, and with good reason. The unnatural activities extended beyond Esther's bedroom. Something hammered on the roof and hurled potatoes around the basement. The knocking sounds took on a strange pattern and seemed to be an attempt at communication. It appeared that whatever was haunting the house was able to hear and see what was going on. When asked questions such as, "How many people are in the room now?" it answered with the correct number of knocks.

In December 1878, Esther became very ill. She spent two weeks in bed fighting diphtheria. Esther's family took very good care of her, but they couldn't help notice that her illness had brought them some blessed relief. Not once during those two weeks did anything unusual happen in the house. When Esther was well enough to travel, she went to stay for a few weeks with another married sister in Sackville, New Brunswick, giving the Amherst household another welcome break from the horror.

But shortly after Esther returned home in early January, things got worse. Along with the noises and moving objects, lit matches would appear out of thin air just below the ceiling and, still burning, drop to the floor. The danger of fire became very real — especially when Esther heard a voice telling her that the house was going to burn down. For the sake of her family, Esther had to go.

Esther's journey over the next several months was a lonely search for peace. Even going to church didn't bring her comfort. She had to stop attending regular Sunday services because the banging and hammering followed her there, disturbing others and leaving her humiliated. The Whites, a farming couple who needed extra help, took her in, but as much as they appreciated how hard she worked, they couldn't deal with the disappearing tools and flying objects.

In March 1879, Captain James Beck played host to Esther in Saint John, New Brunswick. Hoping to learn more about what was happening to her, he invited a group of people interested in after-death connections to meet with Esther and ask the haunting spirit some questions. They concluded that several ghosts were haunting Esther. Another man, Walter Hubbell, reached a similar conclusion.

Hubbell was an American actor who happened to be touring the Maritimes in 1879. Like so many others who had read the newspaper accounts of Esther's nightmare, Hubbell wanted to see for himself what was happening in Amherst. In June, not long after Esther had moved back home, Hubbell showed up at the family's house and was shocked by what he witnessed over the next several weeks. Later he would write a short book, *The Haunted House*, in which he told of a flying umbrella, a whizzing carving knife, chairs that broke on their own and, perhaps most disturbing of all, hundreds of pins that jabbed themselves into Esther's tormented body. Hubbell also reported spending time with Esther when, in a trance-like state, she talked about and even named the many invisible spirits that surrounded her.

At one point Hubbell tried to turn Esther's plight into a moneymaking enterprise. He planned on touring with her, presenting her story as one would a play. But after just one appearance before a disappointed audience, he realized that Esther's ghosts wouldn't make themselves known on demand — something he had hoped would draw big crowds. Hubbell left town soon afterward, but his money-making efforts weren't entirely in vain. His book about what came to be known as "the great Amherst mystery" turned out to be a best-seller.

After Hubbell left, Esther managed to get a job working for an Amherst farmer named Arthur Davison. Like the Whites, the Davisons were willing to put up with a few flying objects and strange sounds — but not unexplained fires. When Davison's barn burned down, he blamed Esther. She was charged with arson, found guilty and sentenced to four months in jail. However, local townsfolk felt sorry for her and convinced authorities to release her after just one month.

Thankfully, by the end of 1879, the spirits that haunted Esther finally left her in peace. Eventually she married a man from Springdale, Nova Scotia, and had a little boy. When her first husband died, she remarried, moved to Massachusetts, and had another son. She died in November 1912, at the age of 52. Several years later, the cottage where the horror began for her was torn down to make way for new shops in downtown Amherst.

But Esther Cox's spirit lives on. The "great Amherst mystery" was written up in books and articles that were published around the world, and her nightmarish experience is still considered one of the most famous ghost stories on record.

MURDER REVEALED

Toronto, Ontario

Russian stonemason Ivan Reznikoff was pleased with his new job in Canada. Like several other foreign stonemasons, he had been encouraged to come to Toronto where his skills were in great demand. In 1858 he was working on the new University College building at the University of Toronto. The money was good, his savings were growing and he was in love. In fact, his girlfriend Susie had just accepted his marriage proposal.

One day, Reznikoff was carving the finishing touches on a large stone head, or gargoyle, that would peer down on passersby when it was done. Several other stonemasons worked alongside him on the detailed carvings that would decorate the upper levels of the building's exterior. During a break, one of the men leaned over and asked Ivan if he recognized the gargoyle that another stonemason, a Greek named Paul Diabolos, was chiselling nearby.

At first glance Ivan didn't notice anything familiar about the head. The figures' mouths usually served as waterspouts draining rain off the roof, and their faces were usually distorted to look rather menacing. But when the man who had spoken to him pointed out that Diabolos was making the gargoyle look like Ivan, the young Russian saw what he meant. There was definitely a resemblance between himself and the Greek's wild-eyed stone creation. But why would Diabolos do this? Ivan wondered aloud. His co-worker replied the Greek was mocking him, because he hadn't realized that his fiancée, Susie, was seeing Diabolos despite her engagement to Reznikoff.

Though Reznikoff was filled with rage, he said nothing. Instead, he spent the rest of the day gouging out new features on his gargoyle to transform it into a hideous sculpture of Diabolos. And that night, armed with an axe, Ivan hid in the bushes near the arched walkway at the university where his informant had said the couple usually met. Right after dark he saw them — Susie and Diabolos — walking hand in hand along the path to the arch. He watched in silence as they sat on a bench and talked, heads close together as if sharing secrets. But when they embraced and kissed passionately, he lost control.

Reznikoff burst from the bushes and raced toward them, swinging the axe. Diabolos jumped up and ran for his life. He dashed into University College and closed the heavy oak door just in time to hear the axe hit it with a thud. He scrambled up a temporary set of wooden stairs in the unfinished stone tower and hid in an alcove. Reznikoff followed, but when he climbed out on the top platform, Diabolos lunged at him with a knife. After stabbing the Russian, he pushed Reznikoff over the edge of the platform and into the 25-metre-deep well where the tower's stone steps were to go.

Diabolos might have been able to make a good case for self-defence, but there's no record of that happening. There's also no evidence that anyone even bothered to report the unfortunate Reznikoff's sudden disappearance. But in the early 1860s, both professors and students started talking about a tall, handsome stranger they'd seen moving about the campus late at night. A few even said that he carried an axe. Whenever anyone tried to speak with him, he mysteriously disappeared.

One night a student named Allen Aylesworth was returning to his dormitory when he met a young man he didn't recognize. Assuming the fellow was a new arrival on campus, Aylesworth started up a friendly conversation with him. After a few minutes, he invited the stranger back to his room for a drink. After downing a couple of shots of whiskey, the stranger stunned Aylesworth by telling him something unbelievable. He said that his name was Ivan Reznikoff and that he was a ghost. He proceeded to talk about his beloved Susie, her betrayal of him with Diabolos and his horrible death at the hands of the Greek. Then he said goodnight and left.

When Aylesworth awoke the next morning, he remembered his encounter with Reznikoff, but he figured it must have been a bad dream. Ghosts — if they existed — didn't just come up and introduce themselves and join you for a drink. Then Aylesworth looked across the room. There on the table were two glasses and an empty liquor bottle.

Word of Aylesworth's eerie experience spread quickly around the university. From then on, whenever people spotted the ghostly apparition of a tall, heavy-set man around University College, they said it must be Reznikoff. In 1890 that explanation started sounding even more believable when the skeletal remains of a large unidentified male were dug up during construction near the base of the college tower. And when old records turned up showing that two stonemasons named Reznikoff and Diabolos had indeed worked at the college, more people became convinced that Aylesworth's tale must have been true. Anyone who still doubted Aylesworth's credibility as a witness, may have had second thoughts when he became a member of Parliament and was later knighted.

Then there's the gouge in the old oak door, said to be made by Reznikoff's axe. It's still there for all to see. And off to one side, glaring down from above, are two expertly carved stone gargoyles.

University College's gargoyles. Could these be the faces carved by Reznikoff and Diabolos?

GHOST TRAIN

Buchans, Newfoundland and Labrador

In late 1927, the American Smelting and Refining Company finished work on a 35-kilometre railway line between Buchans and Millertown in Newfoundland's interior. The company built the line to ship the zinc, lead and copper ores dug out of the Lucky Strike mine in Buchans.

Soon after the line opened, the nearby Buchans River Dam burst, and surging water washed out the wooden train trestle across the river. Over the years, there were other accidents along the line, some of which claimed the lives of men who worked for the mining company. It's said that the spirits of those dead men might have been responsible for reported sightings of a ghost train in the area.

A few years after the Buchans line went into operation, people started talking about seeing a strange, distant light moving along the rails. Of course, it was much scarier for people who were on a train than for those who were standing off to the side of the tracks. That's because as the lights of the phantom train drew closer, it would appear as though another train was heading for a collision with the real one. At the very last second, just as the two trains seemed doomed to crash, the unidentified train would disappear.

Every now and then similar incidents were reported on other train lines in the province. There was also the occasional story about a ghostly conductor on a passenger train.

Today trains no longer operate in Newfoundland. The last one stopped running in 1989, and there haven't been any recent reports of ghost train sightings. But most of the tracks are still in place. What's to stop a phantom train from riding the rails through the Newfoundland backwoods even now? Might it happen again? Only time will tell . . .

THE WOMAN IN BLACK

Johnville, New Brunswick

On May 3, 2001, fire destroyed the Keenan covered bridge near Johnville, New Brunswick. Local residents were sad to lose such a vital part of the area's history. The wooden bridge had been built across the Monquart River in 1927 to replace the original covered span at that location. Many people were also saddened to think that something else had been lost to the flames — the ghost that had haunted both bridges for more than a hundred years.

Stories about the ghost began circulating in the late 1800s, when an older lady entered the bridge one day and was never seen again — at least, not alive. After her disappearance, people started talking about seeing a strange woman wearing old-fashioned black clothes on the bridge. She never spoke to anyone, and she never stayed around when someone tried to approach her.

But the woman in black didn't seem to mind being the one to do the approaching. Silently, mysteriously and without any warning, she would suddenly appear in a wagon or sleigh — or in later years, even a car — sitting *beside* the person who was driving across the bridge. She would sit stiffly upright, staring forward with glazed, unseeing eyes. Worse still, sometimes she was headless.

To find oneself riding with such an apparition could be an absolutely terrifying experience. One farmer was crossing the bridge to visit his sister when he suddenly realized the woman in black was sitting right beside him on the wagon seat. He was frozen with fear. The reins hung limply in his hands, but his horse kept going. Then, as the wagon turned into his sister's lane on the other side of the bridge, he fainted.

When the man came to, the ghostly woman was gone and the horse was panicking. He pulled on the reins to stop the frightened beast, leaped off the wagon and rushed into his sister's house. But he was so stunned by what had happened that it took him a week to find the courage to talk about it.

Several people who encountered the woman in black were like that man. They didn't like talking about what they had seen. So, when Keenan Bridge was burned beyond repair, they must have been relieved. Surely, the ghost was gone forever. But imagine what they thought when they saw a photograph of the burned-out bridge that was taken by a transportation department worker. There, on a piece of smouldering timber, was the haunting image of a woman's face. Shortly after that picture was taken, the face on the charred timber disappeared.

A new bridge has been built across the Monquart River near Johnville. Only time will tell if the woman in black will visit it too.

The smouldering remains of Keenan Bridge.
Inset: Can you see a face?

THE TRAVELLING CORPSE

Fort McPherson, Northwest Territories

In 1852 Roderick Ross MacFarlane started working in
the Northwest Territories as a clerk for the Hudson's Bay
Company. He did his job well and quickly worked his
way up through the ranks to become a factor, or manager. It was during MacFarlane's first few years with the
company that he got to know Augustus Richard Peers.
Peers was a successful fur trader who was put in charge
of Fort McPherson, an isolated post north of the Arctic
Circle.

When MacFarlane got the news that Peers had died in
March 1853, he was sad to hear it. He had liked Peers.
He also remembered hearing Peers say that he never
wanted to be buried at Fort McPherson. But that was
exactly what had happened to the trader's remains.

MacFarlane often thought about what the dead man had said, but it would be nearly seven years before he got a chance to honour Peers' wishes. Late in 1859, he was at Fort McPherson on company business. Before leaving there for Fort Good Hope, where he was factor at the time, MacFarlane decided to take Peers' remains with him.

It wasn't easy digging the coffin out of the frozen ground, but the men assigned to the task finally managed to do it. However, when they hauled the coffin up, they saw that the years had taken their toll. Quickly they built a new, stronger casket. Then they opened the old one. Thanks to the chilly climate, Peers looked much the same as the day he had died. After getting over their shock at seeing how well-preserved the body was, the men carefully moved it to the new coffin, nailed the box shut and tied it to a sled.

After weeks of guiding dog teams and loaded sleds across rugged ice and through blinding snow, MacFarlane and his assistants finally reached Fort Good Hope early in 1860. But their journey wasn't over yet. All along, MacFarlane had planned to rebury Peers at Fort Simpson, which was still nearly 300 kilometres away. After he spent a few days accounting for furs they had picked up along the way, he got ready to hit the trail again. His men had nearly finished loading the sleds with supplies and trade goods for the next part of the journey when they realized there wasn't enough room for Peers' coffin. They removed his body from the box, wrapped it in a blanket and tied it to a sled. Then they were off again.

MacFarlane continued south along the Mackenzie River. The small group of travellers rested for a few days at Fort Norman (now Norman Wells) while MacFarlane conducted some more business. Then they continued moving south.

It was on March 15, 1860, the seventh anniversary of Peers' death, that the men started to feel very uncomfortable. They were setting up camp for the night close to the riverbank when the dogs started acting skittish. Then they began yelping and barking for no apparent reason. A little while later, the men started hearing voices, or more specifically, one voice. Time and again it called out from the darkness. "March," it said. "March."

MacFarlane and his crew searched the surrounding bush, but couldn't find the mysterious caller. They couldn't find what was continuing to upset the dogs, either. The animals kept barking and pawing the ground nervously, ignoring all efforts to calm them. Then, suddenly, they stopped shifting around, curled up and went to sleep. After calming their own nerves, the men finally fell asleep too.

The men heard the ghostly command to "march" once more before their journey ended. Later, MacFarlane would learn that Peers had used that word to urge on his dog team. Was the phantom voice that of Peers, urging the factor to keep moving until his remains were finally laid to rest? MacFarlane thought so, especially after Peers' ghost appeared to him when the group finally reached Fort Simpson. He was so terrified when he sensed the apparition's presence in his room that he hid under the covers in bed until it left.

MacFarlane arranged for Peers' remains to be buried in the Hudson's Bay Company cemetery at Fort Simpson. He stood by the grave as the body was lowered into the ground on March 23, 1860. But for years afterwards, he wondered if he had done the right thing. Were the ghostly cries a sign that Peers' spirit was eager to arrive at Fort Simpson? Or were they cries of complaint because his spirit was upset at having his grave disturbed in the first place? Whatever it was, MacFarlane was relieved when the ghost was still once more.

THE GHOST CHILD

Montreal, Quebec

Sir Arthur Conan Doyle, the creator of the fictional super-sleuth Sherlock Holmes, was very interested in ghosts and in communicating with the spirits of the dead. He often travelled to different cities in North America, giving lectures about the subject. In 1922, he visited Montreal as part of a Canadian lecture tour. There he read a newspaper article about a local couple coping with the presence of a poltergeist. Conan Doyle visited the couple, and what he learned about the haunting made such a strong impression on him that he wrote about it when he returned to England.

The middle-aged couple lived alone in their home, so when strange things started happening, they either had to blame each other or accept the fact that some unearthly force was at work. The man was slower to accept that fact than the woman was — not because he thought she was playing tricks on him, but because he didn't believe in ghosts.

So, when the lights went out time and again, suddenly plunging the house into darkness, he tried to convince her the wiring was faulty. When she was upset to find all the pictures in the house had been taken off the walls, he was curious, but not too worried about how that had happened. But when some invisible hand walloped him with a pillow on two separate occasions, his wife's belief that there was a ghost in their home no longer seemed so silly.

Conan Doyle recorded other eerie incidents that plagued the couple. The woman had kept a box of wooden blocks that their child had played with many years earlier. Several times, either when they got up in the morning or returned to the house together, the couple would be greeted with impressive block towers and buildings. Time after time, they would dismantle the structures and pack the blocks back in the closet, only to find them hauled out and stacked back up, as if a youngster had been having great fun playing with them.

Further evidence that the ghost might have been a child was babyish writing on bits of paper that mysteriously appeared in every room. However, other pieces of paper, covered with clearer lettering and detailed drawings, started showing up too, leading the owners and Conan Doyle to believe that two ghosts — a child and an adult — might be active in the house. Just thinking about such a possibility made the woman more nervous than ever.

The man arranged for a priest to visit and say prayers to drive out any unnatural forces that might be present in the house. But the haunting activity continued, and the couple finally decided they had no choice but to move. Fortunately for them, as Conan Doyle noted, the ghosts didn't move with them, and, after months of stress and fear, they finally found peace in a new home.

THE DOCTOR IS IN

Helmcken House, Victoria, British Columbia

Museums are like windows that offer views of times and places long past. Old houses that have been turned into museums are especially fascinating. As you move through their historically furnished rooms, you can imagine the people who lived there going about their daily tasks. Items such as dishes on the tables and handmade quilts on the beds give the impression that their original owners are expected back any minute.

Maybe imaginations work overtime in old places like these. Whatever the reason, it's not all that unusual for people touring them to report seeing and hearing some pretty spooky things. Helmcken House in downtown Victoria is an old house that has been turned into a museum. It gives visitors a taste of what life in British

Columbia was like about 150 years ago. Apparently some visitors have also experienced enough strange sights and sounds that the place is said to be haunted.

Helmcken House is the oldest house in British Columbia still in place on its original foundations. It started out as a three-room log home built by Dr. John Sebastian Helmcken in 1852. Dr. Helmcken had trained as a doctor in England, and came to Canada as a ship's surgeon for the Hudson's Bay Company. It was also as a doctor for the company that he settled at Fort Victoria. There, Helmcken fell in love and married Cecilia Douglas, the daughter of the colony's governor, Sir James Douglas. It was for Cecilia that the doctor built the first part of what was to become a large, stately home, and later, a museum.

Dr. Helmcken died in 1920, at the age of 96. His youngest daughter, Edith, who had gone to live with him after her husband died in 1896, continued to live in the house until her death in 1939. Soon after, the British Columbia government bought the house and, in 1941, opened it as a museum. Soon after that, the reports of unusual happenings began.

Every now and then someone sees a woman looking out a window on the second floor — even though there's no one in the house. Helmcken's wife, Cecilia, loved her new home, but she didn't get to live in it for very long. She died when she was just 31. It's said that she couldn't bear to leave the house forever, and that she's the woman in the window. There have also been reports of piano music coming from the house when it's empty.

Strange things happen when staff and visitors are in the house too. For example, lights go on by themselves, dishes are moved around the kitchen and thick, heavy doors swing open on their own.

Marc Vermette, a manager at the house, figures Dr. Helmcken and Edith are the invisible spirits who are making their presence known. Over the years he's come to think of them as friends. But a few unsuspecting workers and visitors have been very disturbed by their encounters with the ghosts of Helmcken House, and, for them, one visit to the museum has been one visit too many.

A person investigating the strange events at Helmcken House, stands before the old piano that is said to play by itself. Some people have also pointed out the strange orb of light in this picture that mysteriously floats above the right side of the piano.

THE DUNGARVON WHOOPER

Miramichi, New Brunswick

If you ever heard the blood-curdling, ear-splitting cry of the Dungarvon Whooper, you wouldn't be easily convinced that the story behind the baleful moan was just a legend. Instead, you'd most likely join the ranks of those who've said over the years, "I heard it. It's true. There really is a ghost roaming the banks of the Dungarvon."

There are at least two versions of the story behind those horrible sounds, but the basic details are the same. Apparently sometime around 1860, a young man known only by his last name, Ryan, signed on to be the cook at a logging camp near the Dungarvon River, a branch of the Main Renous River in New Brunswick. Ryan was a friendly, outgoing fellow, well liked by the other loggers. He was also a bit too trusting for his own good. He made no secret of the fact that he kept his savings in a money belt he wore around his waist.

Every morning Ryan would make breakfast for the men. When it was ready, he would let out a loud, whooping yell to wake them up. Then he would pack their lunch pails and, after they left, set about baking and preparing supper.

One day, the foreman stayed behind with Ryan. What happened next depends on who's telling the story. One version has the boss murdering Ryan for his money, hiding his body under the snow and telling the other men that the cook had left while they were gone.

The more popular version has the foreman murdering Ryan for his money in the bunkhouse. When the other men returned to camp and found the young man's body on the floor, the boss told them Ryan had suddenly become ill and died. A fierce winter storm blew in that evening, piling up metre-high snowdrifts that stopped the crew from taking Ryan's body out of the bush for a proper funeral. The men were forced to bury his corpse in a shallow grave in the bush.

That night was a living hell for the men at the camp. The first nerve-wracking whoops pierced the silence of the forest shortly after dark. As the night went on, the horrifying wails grew louder, making sleep an impossibility. By morning the men had had enough. Convinced that they were hearing the mournful cries of the dead Ryan, they packed up and left the camp, vowing never to return.

Apparently, the foreman got away with murder, but it's as if Ryan's ghost found a way to make sure no one forgot his tragic end. For years afterwards, people reported hearing hair-raising screams if they found themselves near the place where Ryan was said to have been buried.

There were even reports of a ghost-like figure rising from the ground, screeching and wailing, if someone stepped too close to the supposed gravesite. Some sightings have the ghost swooping closer and closer until it hovers just overhead, filling the air with ear-splitting wails.

In the early 1900s a local priest, Father Edward Murdoch, travelled to the spot known as Whooper Spring and blessed the area to bring peace to Ryan's troubled soul — and to the people terrified by the unearthly sounds. Some say the prayers worked, and that the woods around the gravesite were quiet at last. Others say that wasn't the case, and that reports of the haunting screams still continue to filter out of the forest.

The Dunvargon Whooper is probably New Brunswick's most famous ghost. In 1912 Michael Whelan, known as the Poet of Renous, published a ballad called *The Dungarvon Whooper.* In it he recounted all the details about the ghost that he'd heard over his lifetime. And a train that ran through the region until 1936 also kept the story of Ryan's murder in people's minds. Perhaps it was because the train was often loaded with rowdy lumberjacks, whooping it up as they went to and from the bush. Or maybe it was because of the haunting sound the whistle made as the train rumbled by. Whatever the reason, the train was known as the Dungarvon Whooper.

RESCUE FROM THE GRAVE

Fox River, Nova Scotia

As a sea captain, George Hatfield was often away from his home at Fox River, west of Parrsboro, for months at a time. In March 1876, he was still a few weeks from home, sailing north from Cuba to Boston in stormy Atlantic waters. After a harrowing day at the helm, Hatfield decided to go below for some much-needed sleep. Soon after he nodded off, he felt a hand on his shoulder and heard someone tell him to alter his course. But when he rolled over and looked around his cabin, there was nobody there.

Hatfield figured his first mate must have left right after delivering his message, so he headed back up to the bridge to find out what was going on. When he got on deck, he found his mate at the wheel, carefully steering the ship through the treacherous waves. Hatfield asked the man why he didn't want to follow the course that had been set, but the mate had no idea what his captain was talking about.

Hatfield felt more than a little foolish. Deciding that he must have dreamed the visitor to his cabin, he went below and stretched out on his bunk again. But once more his sleep was interrupted in exactly the same way. Angry, he went back up to ask the first mate why he wanted to change course and why he hadn't stayed to discuss the matter after waking him up. The poor mate said he hadn't left his post, nor had any other member of the crew.

Confused, Hatfield tried once more to get some rest. He had barely closed his eyes when he again felt someone tapping his shoulder and ordering him in a firm, loud voice to make a specific course change. This time, though, when the captain looked up, he saw a man he didn't recognize leaving his cabin. He jumped up and hurried back up the stairs. When he reached the first mate, he asked him if he had just seen someone walking along the deck. The mate said no. Hatfield looked around for a few seconds, then turned to the worried man and ordered him to alter the ship's course in the way the voice had described. Then the captain returned to his cabin and fell into a deep sleep.

The mate was afraid his captain might be suffering from extreme exhaustion, but he did as he was told. He was still steering the new course when Hatfield appeared back on deck the next morning, looking rested but anxious. Hatfield ordered his crew to keep a close watch on the sea ahead. A few hours later he heard a cry that he seemed to be expecting. One of his men had spotted a battered ship that appeared to be taking on water at a deadly rate.

Through a series of dangerous manoeuvres, Hatfield and his crew managed to get close enough to the American schooner *D. Talbot* to rescue everyone on board. The schooner's captain, a man named Amesbury, was especially grateful to Hatfield. His wife and child were among those rescued.

After Amesbury and his family had dried off and had a warm drink, Hatfield sat down with them and told them how he had found them. As he was describing the strange man who had mysteriously appeared in his cabin, Mrs. Amesbury interrupted him and asked for more details about what the man looked like and what he was wearing. Then she started to cry. When Hatfield asked her what was wrong, she told him he had just described her father. In a trembling voice she went on to explain that her father had died ten years earlier.

Is it possible that Mrs. Amesbury's father cared for her so much that he'd returned from the grave to save her from certain death? Who else could have appeared to Hatfield in the middle of the Atlantic and guided him to the exact spot, in that vast ocean, where his help was needed the most?

THE PROSPECTOR'S SPECTRE

O'Brien Creek, Yukon Territory

Fred Nelson looked as if he had seen a ghost. That's because he had — just a few days earlier. Even back in the safety of Dawson, he was still filled with fear as he spoke of what had happened at the mouth of O'Brien Creek, near what came to be known as Fortymile.

A reporter with the Klondike Nugget carefully observed Nelson as he told his horrifying tale. He noted how Nelson's eyes had a wild look about them, and his hands trembled. His voice even cracked as he gave a detailed account of what he and another gold prospector, a man called Swanson, had seen and heard in a two-room cabin in the wilderness. By the time Nelson had finished his story, the reporter was convinced that it was true. No man could pretend to be that scared.

Like most people in the area back then, Nelson and Swanson had heard rumours that the cabin was haunted. It had sat abandoned for 14 years, ever since its owner, a prospector named La Salle, had been found dead there in 1886. From the bloodied state of La Salle's body, it was clear that he had been murdered. Suspicion had fallen on some Tanana natives from Alaska who were fed up with the fur traders, miners and missionaries that kept invading their territory. However, there was no proof that the Tananas had killed La Salle, and no one was ever charged with the crime.

For years after La Salle's death, stories circulated about strange sounds coming from the cabin. Those few daring enough to go near it — natives and non-natives alike — told of being overcome by a creepy feeling as they approached the door. That weird feeling was enough to send them on their way without going inside.

But the temperature had plunged to nearly 40 degrees below zero on the evening that Nelson and Swanson spotted the cabin in the distance. Faced with the very real possibility of freezing to death, they decided to take shelter in it and hope for the best. They were nervous when they went inside, but once they got a small fire going in the old stove, they felt much calmer. Eventually they fell asleep.

At first Nelson thought it was the howl of the wind that woke him up around midnight. But as he rolled over to get comfortable, he heard the sound again. It wasn't the wind and it wasn't coming from outside. It was the sound of someone moaning and it was coming from the back room. Swanson was awake by then. He had heard the moans too.

Nelson jumped up and pushed on the door connecting

the two rooms, but even though it had swung open freely earlier, it was now stuck. Swanson rammed it with his shoulder, but it wouldn't budge. At that point Nelson thought he heard a low voice weakly pleading for help. As he pulled on his parka, he shouted at Swanson to keep trying to open the door. Then he jammed his feet into his boots and headed outside.

Nelson ran around the side of the cabin, intending to break the small window in the back room. But when he got to it, it was filled with an eerie light. Looking inside he saw the misty apparition of a man with a horrible gash on the side of his head. Petrified, Nelson stumbled back into the cabin and, nearly choking with fear, told Swanson what he had seen.

Swanson backed away from the door, no longer wanting to open it. But the moans grew louder, so he edged nearer and, in a loud voice, told whatever was in the room to identify itself. Over the next several minutes, he asked questions and got patterns of knocks in reply. When Swanson asked if the phantom was La Salle's ghost, the knocks got louder, and when he asked the spirit who had killed him, the door suddenly burst open. Filling the doorway was the glowing image of a man, his arms stretched upwards. Both Swanson and Nelson screamed, but before they could make it outside, the figure vanished.

Both prospectors managed to find the courage to stay in the cabin long enough to pack up their gear. Then they slipped out into the darkness, preferring to take their chances with the deadly cold rather than spend another minute in the shelter of La Salle's cabin.

PHANTOM OF THE EMPRESS

Fort Macleod, Alberta

Fort Macleod is the oldest town in Alberta. About 160 kilometres south of Calgary, it's where the North West Mounted Police (now the Royal Canadian Mounted Police) built their first post in the province in 1874. A reconstruction of the original fort is the town's main tourist attraction.

Fort Macleod is also home to the Empress Theatre, the province's longest operating live theatre. Since opening in 1912, the theatre has always been one of the town's main gathering places. Variety shows, concerts, musicals, plays and lectures — the Empress has hosted them all. It's also been *the* place to go to take in the latest hit movie.

But every now and then the Empress Theatre plays host to an eerie performance that isn't on the list of scheduled events. It's a one-person show, starring a character that theatre staff call Ed. Who Ed is remains a mystery, and what he does is very mysterious too. Those who've seen him say he's a big, hairy fellow who holds his trousers up with suspenders. One show manager reported seeing him in the audience, sitting in the same place in the balcony several nights running. An actor said that Ed actually stood on the stage for a while during an evening performance. And once a customer said he bought tickets from an older, rather large man he didn't recognize, only to learn later that no men were working in the box office that particular night.

Some people say that Ed must be the ghost of a janitor who worked at the theatre more than 70 years ago. No one knows how that man died, but apparently he smoked and drank a lot. He also worked part-time at a local cattle auction. That could explain why smells of tobacco, alcohol and manure linger in the air whenever the ghost makes an appearance. When it once looked as though the Empress would have to close, the sound of crying could be heard in empty dressing rooms. Perhaps the Empress's most faithful janitor couldn't bear to have the theatre close.

Of course, if Ed is the spirit of a long-dead janitor, he seems to have forgotten how hard it is to take care of a theatre. Supposedly he's the culprit who occasionally tosses trash out onto the floor, right after it's been put in the garbage can. He is also blamed for hiding things, setting off the security alarms, slamming doors and flipping the seats up and down. People have also reported hearing someone running in the aisles, even though they can't see anyone there.

Theatre managers say that Ed is a harmless ghost whose antics can be annoying at times. But wouldn't you feel more scared than annoyed if you saw coffee mugs moving around on a table when no one was touching them? And what would you think if you saw footprints forming in a sawdust-covered floor, as if some invisible person were walking across the room? Ed is said to have been responsible for both of those spooky performances.

One theatre patron also said that the image of a stranger suddenly appeared behind him in the mirror — when he was alone in the washroom. When he described the apparition to the staff, they agreed that it sounded just like Ed. But that's the only time he's been seen in the washroom, so theatregoers shouldn't be afraid to use the facilities at the Empress. Still, no one can be sure where or when Ed might show up next. Unlike other performers at the theatre, Ed doesn't advertise his appearances ahead of time.

WAILS OF SORROW

Signal Hill,
Newfoundland and Labrador

Signal Hill in St. John's is one of Newfoundland and Labrador's best-known landmarks. Hike to the top of it and you'll be rewarded with spectacular views of the city and harbour below, the rugged coastline on either side of the narrow harbour entrance and the seemingly endless stretch of ocean beyond it. You'll also have a chance to tour Cabot Tower, the tall castle-like museum on top of the hill. It was built in 1897 to celebrate the 400th anniversary of John Cabot's arrival in the New World.

Signal Hill is also the place where, on December 12, 1901, inventor Guglielmo Marconi received the first trans-Atlantic wireless radio signal. But that's not why the steep rocky rise is called Signal Hill. From the early 1700s, flags that identified approaching ships were flown from a post on the hill to signal to the traders and dockworkers below which ships would soon be sailing into the harbour.

Over the centuries Signal Hill has also played an important role in Newfoundland's defence. It was the ideal place to position batteries — groups of cannon — that could be aimed at any invading ships that tried to enter the harbour. At different times barracks were also built on the hill to house garrisons of soldiers and their families. Scaffolds were erected on the hill too. The shocking sight of hanged criminals dangling high above the port served as a powerful reminder of the price to be paid for crimes such as treason and murder.

With such a colourful history, it shouldn't come as a surprise to learn that a ghost is said to haunt Signal Hill. What may be surprising is that the ghost is believed to be female. Many times people have reported hearing the mournful wail of a woman. The sadness in her cry is unmistakable. But who might she be?

One possible explanation is that she was the wife of a young soldier stationed at one of the barracks on the hill in the early 1840s. Those barracks were terrible places to live in the winter. Constantly battered by icy winds, they were almost impossible to keep warm. In an 1842 report Governor John Harvey referred to "the extreme sufferings" endured by the barracks' soldiers and their families. He described how the chimneys couldn't draw smoke up out of the fireplaces, leaving people with two choices — put out the fires or open the windows to vent the smoke-filled rooms. Either way, the barracks were left bone-chillingly cold.

Things got so bad that more than a dozen frostbitten Royal Artillery soldiers had to be hospitalized. Worse still,

Cabot Tower on Signal Hill

a young mother who had tried to sit up all night holding her baby to keep it warm, woke up the next morning to find it dead in her arms. Harvey was horrified when he found out about the infant's tragic death. He ordered the barracks closed immediately and moved the company down the hill to warmer quarters.

Some say it's the dead baby's mother whose wails have been heard on Signal Hill. But perhaps the heartbroken spirits of other women have also lingered high above the harbour. Many wives and girlfriends used to climb the hill each morning to gaze out at the steely grey Atlantic, hoping for a glimpse of an overdue ship or boat. Often those women waited in vain. Their wails — the cries of women from long ago, whose men were lost at sea — may still blow across the rocky crest of Signal Hill.

SOLDIER FOR ALL ETERNITY

Niagara-on-the-Lake, Ontario

"Swayze's Cellar" — the sign on the wooden plank door says it all. The cellar of the Olde Angel Inn in Niagara-on-the-Lake is Captain Colin Swayze's hangout. The inn's owners don't know when he returned to the basement, but they accept the fact that he has. They even humour him by flying a British Union Jack flag outside. Of course the cellar isn't the most comfortable spot to hang out. Guests have commented how cold it can get down there. But the captain doesn't seem to mind the unusually chilly drafts. He may even be causing them, after all, Swayze has been dead for nearly 200 years.

A British soldier, Swayze fought in Canada against the Americans during the War of 1812. When American invaders showed up at the inn in 1813, Swayze hid in a rum barrel in the cellar. One version of his death has him being killed during a hand-to-hand fight when the enemy found him. Another version has the Americans stabbing him with their bayonets as he crouched in the barrel.

Not long afterward, American forces burned down the inn, and it wasn't rebuilt and expanded until the 1820s. Back then it offered travellers good food, cozy rooms and friendly service. It still does, but over the years it has also offered former and current owners and guests some very strange experiences.

Several years ago a man in a red coat made some sudden appearances — and disappearances — in the women's washroom in front of two startled cleaning ladies. They

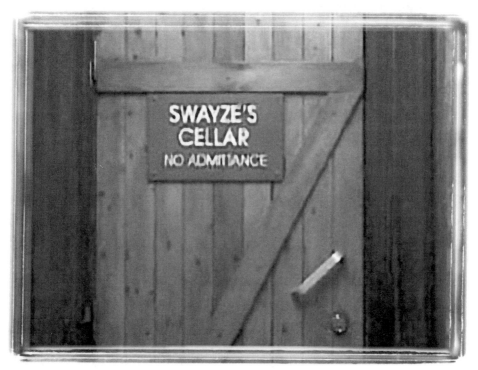

The door to Swayze's Cellar

seem to be the only ones who've actually seen the ghostly figure of an army officer from the past. But Florence LeDoux, a former owner who also lived at the inn as a child, once saw three saucers float through the air, one behind the other, before crashing to the floor several metres away. Her headwaiter, Bruce Cartwright, was nearly hit in the head when a metal beer mug was whipped across the lounge by some invisible hand.

And then there are the footsteps — eerie and plodding — when no one else is around. People have been hearing the footsteps late at night for as long as anyone can remember. There have also been reports of dishes rattling in a cupboard, chairs moving across the floor and the sound of a man's laughter coming from the empty dining room.

Occasionally a guest has heard fife-and-drum marching music coming from a second floor bedroom. No one's been able to discover who — or what — is playing it, but it is the sort of music Captain Swayze and his men would have bravely marched to nearly 200 years ago.

Swayze's death may have stopped him from fighting in the war, but it seems that he will never surrender to death.

THE DEAD LIGHTS

St. Louis, Saskatchewan

St. Louis, Saskatchewan is a small town with a big story to tell. Located about 40 kilometres south of Prince Albert, it's the place to go if you want to hear about — and maybe even see — the St. Louis light.

The ghostly light has been appearing just north of St. Louis for more than 80 years. It shows up often enough that some locals take houseguests out for a midnight drive just to get a glimpse of it. The light rarely lets them down. Young people go out to wait for it too, just for the fun of it. Sometimes, though, seeing it can be more frightening than funny.

Saskatoon residents Serge and Gail Gareau thought it would be entertaining to take friends visiting from Alberta to see the famous light. They arrived in St. Louis about an hour before midnight, and parked outside the town beside the old railway tracks that hadn't been used for years. There was a chill in the air, so they stayed in the car, chatting and waiting. After about an hour, they were ready to head back to Saskatoon. Then it happened. First the light appeared as a small white circle, but then it grew a little larger and brighter and it seemed to get closer and closer. Beneath the white light was a smaller red one.

Amazed, the four friends stayed in the car and watched the lights for more than an hour. It still seemed as though the beams were getting closer, but they never actually did, so Serge and his buddy decided to go toward them and check them out. They started the car and edged out onto a bumpy dirt road that ran beside the old rail line. After they'd been driving for a few minutes, the lights suddenly went out.

But, just a few seconds later, an eerie glow filled the car. All four turned around, and, to their horror, saw that the light was now behind them — and it was much too close for comfort. Amid shrieks and shouts to get out of there, Gareau sped back toward the main road at top speed. As they drove away, they could see that the light was gone again.

Documentary filmmakers, a university professor and even a mayor of St. Louis, Emile Lussier, have all gone on record as having seen the light. Distant headlights have been offered as one explanation for its fairly regular appearance, but Lussier said experts investigated and rejected that possibility. Besides, people were seeing the light as far back as the 1920s, when hardly anyone in the area owned a car.

But trains were still running past St. Louis then, and some locals recall a story about a tragic accident on the tracks near their town. Details are vague, but the story has a worker carrying a lantern as he walked along the tracks checking for loose rails. The unfortunate man was struck by a locomotive, and the blow was so powerful that it ripped off his head.

The train tracks were pulled up years ago, but some people believe that horrifying death scene is still being played out every time the light appears. The white light is the headlight of the engine that hit the man, and the smaller red light is the lantern he was holding when it sent him to his death.

THE VANISHING VISITOR

Summerland, British Columbia

Summerland nestles on the western shore of Okanagan Lake, a few minutes drive north of Penticton. Home now to more than 10 000 residents, it was a small farming community when World War I was raging in Europe. Back then newcomers to the area — many from Manitoba — were still planting thousands of fruit trees in what would soon become Canada's world-famous Okanagan Valley orchards.

One family (whose members wanted to remain anonymous) settled on the outskirts of Summerland and welcomed the valley's peace and quiet even more so as bloody battles were being fiercely fought abroad. The parents were grateful to still have their two boys at home, both because they were safe and because they could help out with all the work that had to be done in the apple orchard.

But one night, as the two young men finished up the day's chores, they felt anything but safe. They had gone out to move their horse to a grassier part of the meadow beside the orchard. While they were re-tying it, a sudden movement in the distance caught the younger brother's eye. Across the pasture, he saw a man walking along the lonely road that ended just past their orchard. Since their family's farm was the last one on the road, the boy couldn't help but wonder where the man had come from. He also wondered who he was.

It was hard to see the man's face clearly in the moonlight, but both brothers felt sure he was a stranger to the area. He was solidly built, and, as he got closer, they saw that he was wearing a white hip-length jacket buttoned high at the neck. It looked a lot like an old-fashioned type of lounge jacket that a country gentleman might have worn years before. The younger brother called out a greeting, and asked where he was going. The man turned, looked right at him, then turned away without saying a word and kept right on walking toward the farmhouse. The boys lost sight of him as he strolled past the front of their house to the side door.

The brothers headed home quickly. They were eager to meet the mysterious night visitor. But when they opened the door into the kitchen, they saw only their parents, sitting at the table. When they asked where the stranger was, their parents looked puzzled. They said no one had come to the door and they had heard no one knocking or walking around outside.

"But that can't be. He was just here," the brothers said, and they explained to their parents what they had seen and heard. Or, more significantly, what they had not heard. It suddenly dawned on the younger brother that the man had not only remained silent when spoken to, but had also not made a sound when he walked. Neither brother had heard a single footstep as the stranger strolled confidently along the road past them on that still, moonlit night.

That the man hadn't spoken wasn't too unusual: he could have simply been rude or unwilling to talk. But no person could walk along a road like that without making a sound. So who, or what, was the man?

In the next few weeks, the brothers casually asked neighbours if they had seen any strangers in the area recently. No one had. The young men never let on why they were asking, because they didn't want folks to guess what they suspected must have happened that evening. Even 40 years later they wouldn't use their real names when they spoke about how the two of them, together, on a quiet, moonlit night, had seen and tried to speak to a ghost.

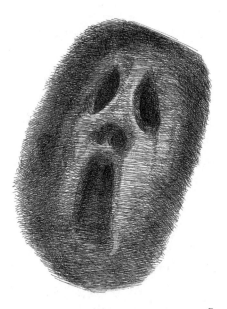

HEADLESS HARVIE

Windsor, Nova Scotia

In the winter of 1906 George Stanley chopped off Freeman Harvie's head and hid the gory remains in his basement. Then Stanley claimed Harvie had left town and given him all his worldly goods, but some folks in Windsor became suspicious. A search of Stanley's place soon turned up the decapitated body. Stanley was charged, tried and convicted of murder, and in the summer of 1906 he was hanged for his crime.

Not long afterward, Judge Charles Edgar DeWolfe reported seeing an apparition of a headless man in a basement window. Knowing that parts of Harvie's corpse had been found hidden under a pile of potatoes in a basement, DeWolfe was certain that what he had seen was the ghost of the unfortunate murder victim. Others who heard his story weren't so sure. But a few days later, DeWolfe became even more convinced that's what had happened.

The judge was walking home, his mind on other things, when an empty barrel appeared out of nowhere. It rolled along Water Street, crossed the road, changed directions, kept on rolling along the sidewalk and then turned sharply on to his front lawn. The judge couldn't believe his eyes. It was as if some invisible hand had been pushing the barrel all the way there. When he caught up to the barrel, he couldn't believe his ears either. Low, mournful groans were coming from the barrel. Then a voice spoke. "I am Freeman Harvie," it moaned. Terrified, Judge DeWolfe steered clear of the barrel and scurried into his house.

From then on, almost every time he went out, the judge came across more evidence of a ghostly visitor. As he passed a few boys on the sidewalk, they suddenly went into zombie-like trances, as did a couple of clerks when he went into stores to shop. The boys and the clerks would stay frozen, eyes staring straight ahead, until the judge — who had done a lot of reading about hypnotism — spoke to them in a soothing voice and waved his hands slowly past their faces. Only then would they snap out of their trances. Before DeWolfe's eyes, old coins would fall from the sky and light bulbs would smash to the ground in front of him. Chairs started rocking on their own when he dropped into the town's furniture factory, and strange voices called out his name. It was as if a mischievous ghost had possessed the entire town.

Judge DeWolfe became more and more concerned about what was happening. In an attempt to find an explanation for the mysterious events, he wrote to an organization that took a scientific approach to investigating claims of ghostly hauntings. He even sent along signed statements from other people in Windsor who claimed that unexplained events had been happening to them as well. That group sent Hereward Carrington, a young reporter and magician, to check out DeWolfe's story.

After DeWolfe gave Carrington a detailed account, they toured some of the places in Windsor where the eerie incidents had occurred. At the grocery store, an apple flew across the room, barely missing Carrington's head. Carrington was amazed, but still not convinced some unearthly force had moved it. He couldn't help noticing that even though the grocer's hands were on the counter, the shopkeeper blushed when the apple took off. At the furniture factory, Carrington listened carefully as sincere-sounding workers explained how they'd been just as frightened as the judge when chairs spontaneously fell over and the pipes started making weird knocking noises. Suddenly Carrington himself was startled by some rocking chairs that began to move back and forth on their own.

Excited by the possibility of finally finding real evidence of a poltergeist's presence, Carrington still took time to examine the rocking chairs very carefully. That's when he found the first signs of human, not ghostly, hands. Behind the chairs he found a hole in the floor. Coming out of the hole was a string that had been looped through each of the chairs. One pull from the basement below could start all the rockers moving.

But Carrington said nothing about what he had found and continued touring the factory. Pipes started banging, furniture fell over and coins dropped to the floor. One man even went into a trance, but Carrington noted that the supposedly frozen fellow had trouble stifling a laugh. The reporter was now certain that he was observing pranksters at their best, but he still said nothing to the unfortunate judge.

However, when the two men moved on to other shops in town, various culprits decided to tell the truth. One young woman admitted to throwing some paper to the floor in the stationery store, and two young men confessed they had just been pretending when the judge had found them acting like zombies. But Judge DeWolfe wouldn't believe them.

When Carrington decided to go out again without the judge, more people came forward to tell him that they had also been in on the joke. For that's what it had been — a practical joke played at the expense of Judge DeWolfe. It had all started innocently enough when two boys who were playing with the barrel let it get away from them. When they saw how alarmed the judge was by the runaway barrel, they decided to play a trick on him. They, like the rest of the town, knew that the judge had claimed to see the headless ghost. Before he got to his front gate, one of them hid in the barrel, moaned and groaned and said he was Freeman Harvie.

When DeWolfe reported Harvie's second appearance, the boys bragged about what they had done. After that, more people came up with other mischief-making schemes, assuming the judge would quickly figure out what was going on. But he didn't. Even when he read Carrington's final report on the nature of the "haunting" weeks later, he clung to his interpretation of what had happened. Perhaps he had trouble accepting the facts because his feelings would have been so hurt if they were true. But maybe there was another reason for his reluctance. After all, he had seen the headless ghost in the window, and Carrington was never able to disprove that eerie appearance.

A PARANORMAL PRESENCE

Gagetown, New Brunswick

In 1941 M. Patricia Jenkins, one of Canada's best-known weavers, bought a large two-storey house in Gagetown, New Brunswick. Called Roseneath, the house had been built in 1810 by Hugh Johnston Jr., a rich local businessman and politician.

Jenkins loved her home, and liked having houseguests. But some of her visitors weren't as comfortable at Roseneath as she was. Several of them felt that there was an invisible presence in the house. One old friend who came for the weekend stayed up all night reading so she wouldn't fall asleep. She not only felt the presence, but also sensed that it wasn't thrilled with her being there. Another visitor told Jenkins she felt the presence as soon as she walked through the door, and she got the impression that a sad-looking, red-cheeked man was standing on the stairs when she arrived.

Jenkins herself had noticed something a little unusual about her house shortly after she moved in. She had decided to replace the dark, rusty-brown wallpaper in the living and dining rooms. After scraping off several layers of old paper, she was amazed to find that the original layer was almost identical to the paper she had bought. At the time she had just thought it was a wonderful coincidence. After some of her friends started talking about the strange feeling they got in her house, she wasn't so sure.

Jenkins started asking questions about Roseneath. The people she had bought the place from told her they had often heard strange noises for which they could find no cause. What's more, a clergyman friend had seen the ghostly apparition of a woman several times when he visited them. Stephen Hall, an elderly gentleman whose parents owned the house in the early 1900s, remembered hearing creepy noises coming from different parts of the house too. He also told Jenkins that there had been stories about eerie lights that moved along the hall and up the stairs to the attic.

Jenkins started seeing Roseneath in a new light. Although she hardly ever sensed a strange presence herself, she accepted the fact that others felt a ghostly spirit also called Roseneath home. But that possibility didn't frighten her; in fact, it was even a little comforting. At least it gave her an explanation for some of the other weird things that happened at the house over the years. For instance, she could blame the ghost's taste in art for the trouble she had trying to hang a new painting.

A group of friends had pitched in to buy the picture for Jenkins, and she wanted to hang it in a place where they could see how much she loved their gift. She chose what she thought was the perfect place for the large forest scene — above the fireplace in the living room. The next morning she found the painting propped up on the mantel. The hook was still securely nailed to the wall and the wire loop attached to the picture frame was still intact, so it was clear that the painting hadn't just fallen down onto the mantel.

Three more times Jenkins tried to hang the painting — on another wall in the living room, above the fireplace in her bedroom and over a low bookcase in the hall upstairs. Each time the painting would be taken down, but not by Jenkins or anyone else visiting her. Finally, Jenkins tried hanging the painting in the living room again, on a wall opposite the windows that looked out on the yard. The next morning, the picture was still in place. It was never moved again.

Did the mysterious presence in the house want the picture hung where she couldn't see it? Or did she want it hung where she could look in at it if she were outside in the garden? There was a spot in the yard where, despite every gardening effort, absolutely nothing ever grew. Jenkins used to joke that the bare spot might be where her invisible housemate did her exercises. But perhaps the resident spirit did spend time outside and liked to see the painting from her favourite spot in the garden.

Jenkins didn't worry too much about why the painting was moved. She wasn't even seriously worried about whether or not her house was haunted. After all, she never actually saw any ghostly figure roaming around Roseneath. She admitted that she often turned around because she felt someone had just come into the room, only to find no one there. But she figured that sort of thing happened to everybody, no matter where they lived.

But did everybody else's cat act the way hers did when that sort of thing happened? Did their pets suddenly look up, eyes large with fear, and slowly turn their heads as if they were watching someone move around the room? Did they act as if they had just seen a ghost? Jenkins' cat did, and she couldn't help but wonder why.

A GHOST NIGHT'S SLEEP

Winnipeg, Manitoba

Like most grand old hotels, the Fort Garry Hotel in Winnipeg has strong links with the past. It was built in 1913, close to where Upper Fort Garry once stood. The fort was built way back in 1835, on the site of an earlier trading post. In 1870 the famed Metis leader, Louis Riel, captured it during the Red River Rebellion.

But a connection to history isn't the only thing many grand old hotels have in common. Like several others, the Fort Garry Hotel is said to be haunted.

For years, guests at the Fort Garry have reported feeling as if they weren't alone when they stayed in certain rooms. But those reports haven't stopped hundreds of guests from returning to the hotel year after year. In fact, a few specifically ask for a room that is rumoured to be haunted.

But what if, one night, the rumour became a reality? Suppose you fell asleep in such a room, and woke up a few hours later because you felt the mattress move, as if someone — or something — had lain down beside you? Would you just tell yourself you were dreaming and fall back asleep?

That's what Brenda Chamberlain, a member of parliament from Ontario, did when that happened to her at the Fort Garry. About 30 minutes later, Chamberlain woke up again. This time she had felt the invisible presence shift its weight on the mattress, as if it were trying to get more comfortable. At that point, a more timid person might have grabbed a robe and headed down to the main desk to demand a new room. But Chamberlain didn't. Somehow she managed to stay calm, and even got a few more hours of sleep.

Chamberlain was lucky, though. She probably wouldn't have stayed so calm if she had seen what some housecleaning staff say they've seen in one second floor room — streaks of blood running down the walls. And she might have been at least a little upset if a woman in a long white dress had floated at the end of her bed before drifting out the window. That's what one guest said she saw when she stayed at the hotel.

A story about a doomed couple in love may explain the presence of haunting spirits at the Fort Garry. It's said that a young woman ran away years ago to stay with her boyfriend at the hotel. Her father and brothers supposedly found the couple there and murdered the boyfriend. Crazed with grief, the young woman hanged herself in the closet. Another similar story has a young woman hanging herself in the closet after finding out that her husband had just been killed in a car accident.

The Fort Garry Hotel

Whatever the reason for her suicide, the grief-stricken young woman is said to wander the hotel in search of her lover. Some people believe that she died in the room where the blood appears on the walls and that she's the woman in the white gown. Could she or her boyfriend also be the ghostly visitor who slips into guests' beds? Some people say yes, and that the two lovers are trying to find each other and be together again.

But the story of the dead couple doesn't seem to explain what happened at the hotel back in 1989. Two staff members were cleaning up the kitchen after 3 a.m. when they heard a noise in the dining room. The room was locked up for the night, and there wasn't supposed to be anyone in there. Quietly, the two men pushed open the swinging door from the kitchen. What they saw surprised them. Sitting at a table was a man who seemed to be thoroughly enjoying eating the dinner set out in front of him. They had never seen him before, and they hadn't served him any food.

The workers slipped out to the front desk to ask the night manager if he knew who the man in the dining room was. He had no idea what they were talking about. Curious, he went back to the kitchen with them and pushed open the swinging door. The dining room was dark and silent, and there was no sign of the man or the food he'd been eating.

Was that middle-of-the-night diner another ghostly visitor checking into the Fort Garry Hotel? Perhaps. Who else could he have been?

FRIGHTENED TO DEATH

Scotchfort, Prince Edward Island

People keep on talking about some strange and scary events long after they happen. What happened to Peter MacIntrye was so terrifying that some people still talk about it more than 200 years later.

MacIntyre was one of the hundreds of Highlanders who sailed from Scotland in the late 1700s in search of a better life. Like many others, his destination was Prince Edward Island, known back then as St. John's Island. The last stop on his voyage was a place named Scotchfort, about 30 kilometres north of Charlottetown.

For MacIntyre and the other new arrivals, life was hard but it was good. They quickly settled in, clearing land, building houses and planting crops. Before long, they began to feel right at home.

One evening, MacIntyre decided to head over to the general supply store where local men often gathered for a chat. Just as he had hoped, he found a few of his neighbours sitting around the wood stove, talking about work and sharing family news. At one point, according to the story folks still tell, a man named Ben Peters brought up the business of the old French cemetery nearby. Many people already believed that the spirits of the dead weren't exactly resting in peace there. So, when Peters said that he had seen a big fiery ball of light drifting over the graveyard, no one was too surprised. No one, that is, except MacIntyre.

Still a relative newcomer, MacIntyre hadn't heard all the rumours about the strange goings-on in the cemetery. And even if he had, he probably wouldn't have believed them. Silly superstitions about the dead didn't frighten him, and he made it clear that evening that he wasn't about to be spooked by tales like the one Peters had just told. But the other men were. Peters' description of the eerie light floating over the graves had sent chills down their spines.

Still, they didn't want to look like cowards in front of MacIntyre. So, instead of admitting they were afraid, they decided to dare him to prove that he wasn't. If, as he claimed, there were only dried out, silent, unmoving bones in the cemetery, then he shouldn't be afraid to spend some time there at night.

MacIntyre said he wasn't the least bit frightened to take their dare. In fact, he added, he'd do it that very night. To make sure he really went, one man grabbed a pitchfork leaning against the wall and handed it to MacIntyre. He told MacIntyre to jam it into the ground in the middle of the graveyard. The men agreed that if they found it there the next day, they'd give MacIntyre a large pouch of tobacco. Saying he looked forward to filling his pipe with his prize,

MacIntyre headed out into the darkness, pitchfork in hand.

The next day, a few of the men set out for the cemetery. On the way, they passed MacIntyre's place. They called out to him, but the only answer they got was the noise of hungry farm animals waiting to be fed. MacIntyre wasn't there, and he hadn't been there earlier either, or he would have fed his livestock. Nervously, the men continued on their way, grateful that the sun was still high in the sky. When they got close to the cemetery, they called out MacIntyre's name again.

The silence that greeted them there left them cold. But the sight that awaited them up ahead was far more chilling than they could ever have imagined. It was the pitchfork handle that drew them further into the graveyard. It was sticking straight out of the earth, as if marking the spot beneath. And as they drew closer, they saw what was under it.

There, lying on an old grave, was MacIntyre. His eyes were wide open and his mouth was twisted in fear. The men stumbled towards him, ready to help if they could.

But MacIntyre could not be helped. When one man touched his hand, it was cold and stiff. MacIntyre had been dead for hours, and from the look on his face, it was clear that his had not been a peaceful death. Fighting off the horror swelling inside them, the men bent down to pick up MacIntyre's body, but they couldn't lift it. Only then did they notice that the pitchfork had been driven into MacIntyre's long coat, spread out on the ground beneath him.

Someone — or something — had jammed that pitchfork into the ground after MacIntyre had dropped to the ground. But who? Or what? That's the question some folks still ask over 200 years later.

PHOTO CREDITS

The publisher thanks the following for providing photographs:

Page 8, Illustrated London News and Picture Library

Page 15, courtesy of Fort Calgary

Page 23, Johan Adlercreutz, Out There, Adlercreutz Photo & Reportage

Page 39, courtesy of W. Lambert (Scot) Gardiner

Page 55, courtesy of Neil Hill

Page 64, courtesy of Rod Vessey, Valley Paranormal Investigations

Page 71, courtesy of Dru Oja Jay

Page 82, courtesy of The Olde Angel Inn

Page 101, courtesy of Dee M. Freedman, Hauntings Research Group © 2000